WHEN ONE SAYS YES

POEMS
BY
ANNE HOLME

COCKLESHELL PRESS
1999

First Published in 1999
by Cockleshell Press,
Jasmyn House, Chapel Road,
Southrepps, Norwich, NR11 8UW.

Copyright © : The Estate of
Anne C.M.Earl, 1999

Typeset and Printed by
Express Printing, North Walsham,
Norfolk NR28 0AN
Tel: 01692 406439

ISBN 0 95357401 0 5

CONTENTS

FOREWORD

These poems of my mother's were a revelation to me, in more senses than one. Their virtue lies in their simplicity, and that simplicity, I think, comes from some sort of adamantine vision that Mum seems to have had from early childhood. She has a composite and comprehensive vision of the world, in which God has a major part, but so does the child in her and in all of us, and none of this, as far as she is concerned, should ever be forgotten.

At the same time it is a poetry which takes on the demanding complexities of life, and does not shirk any of its difficulties. She wrestles with her faith, in action and in words, and she is a notable champion of the dispossessed and the downtrodden - ("Mothering Sunday" raised a pang!). Her work says something special to mothers and children, about whom she cared deeply, through the church as well as in teaching - she was trained at a Froebel college, and taught in a school of her own as well as in a school for the handicapped. Her special gift for storytelling, something we all benefited from, is in evidence in many poems, most notably "The Message".

Her work is all of these things, but there is also a delight in words for themselves, without which real poetry is not possible. There is a variety of form and content that is remarkable, and the best of her poetry has that fluidity of word and experience moving together, the "art that conceals art".

We will all have our favourites, but mine are the ones that show another deep aspect of her personality. She knew the countryside in a way that perhaps few can do these days, from that pond in Penn where she found she was to be a poet to the forgotten corners of Norfolk where God speaks in an empty church, and thought, stained wall and crooked timbers are perhaps all the same thing. She knew and loved landscape in detail - and, like her brother Christopher and sister Alix, seemed to have something of a personal relationship with wild flowers! Her love of being inside the landscape is a vital part of her poetry, brought most close, I think, in "Fox", or in that
> "Spire of willowherb, intensest red,
> Holding the key to all."

In the sensuousness with which she approaches nature, the quick-witted realism of her grasp of the spiritual, and the depth of her conviction - tinged with the humour that was inevitably Mum's - that life is worth living and fighting for, Anne Holme has a distinctive and valuable voice. I know I am biased, but I know also that there are few who can bridge the physical and metaphysical with such calm, eloquence and unshakeable faith.

"How many heavy hearts each eventide
Helplessly stand
And watch the little boats drift out to sea
And weep. Yet somewhere, though far off it be,
Those little boats come safe again to land"

John Earl, August 1998

BIOGRAPHICAL NOTE

Anne Holme was born in 1917 at Maymyo in Burma, where her father worked as a member of the Indian Civil Service. She was, as she liked to say, shipwrecked before she was born, because her mother tried to return to Britain for her birth but had to go back to Rangoon when their ship hit a mine off Colombo - an incident which did not prevent Anne from developing a love of sailing, as several of her poems indicate.

After she did get to England, at the end of the war, she spent most of her childhood at Penn, in Bucks., much of it in a community of children whose parents were, like hers, working in Burma. This period, which was a very happy one, is reflected in a number of poems, particularly "Endings" and "Uncle Willie".

She then went to St. Felix School at Southwold - hence "My Field" - and then to the Froebel College at Bedford. She taught at a hospital school - the Heritage School at Chailey in Sussex - and then at various schools in Bucks. as well as running a small school of her own.

In 1943 she married Jack Earl, a schoolmaster temporarily turned Naval Met. Officer, whom she had originally met on a skiing holiday in Austria. After eleven very happy months together in Orkney, Jack went to sea, and they did not see one another for a year and a half.

After the war Jack went back to teaching and then, five years later, became an H.M.I. Married life became a process of moving into new places, settling in and moving on again. They lived in Essex (at Loughton), in Northern Ireland (at Greenisland, near Belfast), in Yorkshire (at Huddersfield), in Derbyshire (at Whatstandwell) and in Berkshire (at Brightwell, near Wallingford). Two children were born in Belfast and two at Huddersfield. In 1972, as retirement approached, they moved to Jack's native Norfolk, living first at Rockland St. Mary, on the Broads, and then at Trunch and Southrepps in the north, near the sea, which they both loved.

While the children were young Anne concentrated her attention on them, though never to the exclusion of wider interests. By the time they left Derbyshire she was travelling all over the county speaking for the Mothers' Union. At Brightwell this continued and she ran several children's activities, including a playgroup and the local Guides, of which she became District Commissioner. It was at Brightwell, too, that she began the Open University course which gave her so much satisfaction.

In Norfolk, to work with the M.U. and with children she added training and work as a Reader in the church - almost as soon as women were admitted to that office (see "Anglican Diversity"). The Open University claimed more and more attention until she graduated, in 1978, with first class honours. She then developed another interest and worked for ten years as a counsellor at the St. Barnabas Centre in Norwich. She completed an academic thesis on Christian and Humanist ideas in counselling less than two years before her death, which came at the beginning of 1998.

Anne had been writing poetry ever since she was a child ("New World") but there is no doubt that she was greatly stimulated by her work with the Open University. Some of the poems ("A 303" and "Wensum Lodge") directly comment on this, but many others, especially the more technical ones, such as "Vowels", reflect the course's influence. Anne often used to say how glad she was that she had delayed her degree course until she was really able to appreciate it. She went on enjoying and writing poems until the very end.

She also maintained an active interest in art throughout her life, and the illustrations reproduced here are all taken from her sketchbooks.

ACKNOWLEDGEMENTS

Acknowledgement is made of earlier publication of the following poems :

"The Port of Norwich", in *Voices*   (Poetry Today, 1996)

"Heraldry", in *Among The Roses* (The Poetry Guild, 1997)

"The Earth Mover", in *Voice And Verbosity* (Poetry Today, 1998)

"You Are The Sun", in *In The Beginning* (Poetry Today 1998)

"No Afterwards", in *de facto* (Poetry Today, 1998)

"When One Says Yes", in *Deo Volente* (Poetry Today, 1998)

ENDINGS

Endings are beginnings.
Beginnings are endings.

There is an oak-tree
At the corner of the field...
For five - no - six years,
Seven-year-olds to twelve-year-olds,
We had played in the garden, climbed the trees
Swung, scrambled, hidden, shouted..
Picked the buttercups, nicked the strawberries,
Raided the nut-trees and the apple store,
Spring, summer, autumn, winter,
Six years' seasons round.

Now it was the last afternoon,
The very last golden afternoon...
A golden September afternoon, getting late
Already the shadows were long across the grass.
And I was in the oak-tree in the corner of the field,
A tree I'd never played in before.

What were we playing?
Camps - shipwrecks? We'd run and shouted
Jumped down the gravel pit, waded in the long grass.
Now I was alone in the tree, exulting.
I watched the clouds over Home Farm brightening,
The sun westering, the shadows lengthening.
It was the very last afternoon
To-morrow we'd all be gone.

Suddenly time ceased. The sun stood still -
Earth slipped her moorings, went spinning into space -
A flash of a second, a millionth of a heartbeat -
(How write it? How tell it?
Words are so clumsy ...)

It was gone. The sun sank.
They called from the house:
"Time to come in now.
You've a journey to-morrow."

To-morrow. To-morrow.
A long way to go.

NEW WORLD

Unmoved, unwaved, unthought-of
- I was coming home from school
Across the common, seven years old;
It was a cool
Summer afternoon, and by the pond,
Quite unthought-of, I suddenly donned
The mantle of a poet
Who didn't (certainly) know it.

Unmoved, unwaved, unthought-of
- I came across the common and round
The pond, balancing on the low stone wall.
There were steps I'd found,
Put there long ago for the chaps
Who got their water here, not out of taps.
Quite unmoved, I trod a secret path
Into other kingdoms, I didn't know where -
Suddenly there.

Unmoved, unwaved, unthought-of
- Seven years old, and suddenly unwrought
Into a different shape, an unknown world.
This was a sort
Of new beginning, though I didn't know
Then, where it might be I'd go,
But walked on home, and said to my Mum:
"I've made a poem - What's for tea?"
Quite unwaved and unthought-of
Was she, was she, was she.

1996

Author's Note (1997): "Unmoved, unwaved, unthought-of" were
the first and third lines of each four-line verse of my first poem, but
I can't remember much more of it. Who was the mysterious
"unmoved" person? I remember the occasion quite well - coming
round the village pond on my way home from school, balancing on
the low stone wall round it. I was ravished by the romance of this
"unwaved" person who "gazed on a silent sea". Perhaps it was
me? The poem ended: "Was she. Was she. Was she", but my mother
was not really as "unmoved" as that - she promptly fetched a new
exercise book with a black, shiny cover, wrote my name on the
front, and wrote down the poem. I wrote all my poems in it for
years*. "New World" is not a bad name for the experience.

*And that book has now been found. Ed.

LEAVES

Leaves, leaves,
    Come on leaves, beat the wind,
        Beat the grey sea-fog, the grey air,
        Palmate, fronded, curly,
            Like fans, like spears,
                Everywhere.

Everywhere unfold -
    Come on leaves, come on out.
        Aren't you in a hurry, you trees,
        Bare towers, cloud-headed, blown
            By the cold spring
                Breeze?

Unfold, uncurl,
    Come on leaves, wake again,
        Wake and wave, stream, ring
        Down the wind, out pennants fling,
            Wake up, hurry up -
                It's Spring!

April 1978

TOM THE PIPER'S SON, HIS FIELD

It was our favourite field,
I don't know why -
A bare slope rising
To meet the sky.

Just a green field
and, just as it should,
Right in the middle grew
a round wood.

Completely round it looked
from the lane below -
Grown to shelter partridges
long ago.

Over that high horizon
mystery yields -
There was just another wood
and further fields.

We only saw the green rise,
the violet hedge
And scudding clouds driving
over the edge.

Or, in autumn, the striped plough
leap to the blue.
And then?... that was the secret
we never knew.

O enticing horizon,
secret to satisfy,
Where a bare field rises
to meet the sky.

Dec.1977

UNCLE WILLIE

Uncle Willie was totally deaf, and when my Aunt
Had secrets to tell him, they had to go out in the car,
Otherwise the whole house would know, the children
In silent ecstasy as she shrieked "Willie!" from afar - and
"Willie!" in agonised entreaty as he reached the point,
The shocking point, of one of his unrespectable stories:
The man who shouted in chapel "This bally eagle won't keep still."
The children (who knew it by heart already)
Savouring afresh its glories,
And egging him on against Aunt Helen's will.

And he explained once, at teatime, exactly how an internal
Combustion engine worked, with all the forks,
Knives and cruets arranged in diagrams to help...
"Willie!" my aunt shrieked, deploring the chaos, not caring
(Though I still know) how an internal combustion engine works.

His car was a Minerva, open, of course;
All the children perched up on the back seat,
Aunt Helen sitting beside him, and vainly shrieking "Willie!"
When he took his hands off the wheel
And, gesticulating, coasted down the long hills,
Shouting "One in four means it drops one foot in every four feet."

On Sundays after tea my aunt read to us
Out of little good books, and afterwards, in the study,
Uncle Willie read "Lorna Doone", "King Solomon's Mines", "She",
"The Chaplet of Pearls", "Coral Island"...it comes back to me, the ruddy
Firelight glancing off the crossed oars, the silver cups, the faded red
Curtains ... and eyes gleaming, opal caverns, delicious terrors lurking
In the shadows behind our circle, waiting till we left the firelight
And went up to bed.

On summer evenings we were out in the field playing cricket.
Uncle Willie named us all after heroes of yore
(Only one of us was ever promoted to be W. G. Grace)
And we had to bowl with a spin, and keep a straight bat,
                                    and <u>never</u> be out leg before.
And as the shadows lengthened across the buttercups
My aunt threw open the window,
Shouting "Willie! Send those children in!"
But we knew we were safe for hours more in the golden evening

For Somerset needed three more runs and Somerset
(Uncle Willie's county) always had to win.

Uncle Willie took us out in the dark - oh splendour
Of silver constellations wheeling round the whole
Dark sky - and their names, names of mystery, names we could savour,
Rolling them round our tongues, - "That's Cassiopieia,
That's Betelgueuse, that's Aldebaran, and look, behind that pole,
The telegraph pole at the top of the drive, that's not a star, that's Mars -
When we get back it will have moved..you can tell."
He went on explaining, while we thrilled to the windy darkness,
The night noises, and the red planet that moved among the stars.

I can't think of any school or anyone who taught me more than Uncle Willie...
More than things - just how endlessly, how, springing
Like a fountain, the whole world is there for us
To drink in learning - unquenched, unstoppable, Pierian Spring.

MY FIELD

I live in the railway age -
The train goes on.

When I was fourteen
I saw from a train
the most wonderful field in the world
and then it was mine.

I saw it again on the next journey
(six times a year I did that journey,
on the L.N.E.R., as it used to be called)
starting in dirty old Liverpool Street Station,
getting in with a crowd of chattering schoolgirls -
back to school.
But the next bit
was a secret.
I never told why I took no notice
between Manningtree and Ipswich
of the gossip and laughter and teasing -
I wanted to see my field.
It had a steep slope down to the railway
and an oak-tree right in the middle
for shelter.
There it is!
Another year's gone - and there it is -
It had trees all round it -
and a spring - with a trough to drink from,
green rushes round the spring,
ox-eye daisies, thistles, campion,
and a little square shelter with a roof,
near the oak-tree -
It had everything.

Later, by chance, I found myself
on the L.N.E.R.,
once a year, bound for holidays on a boat,
happily excited as we chugged along.
Yes - there it is...
I have left school - but my field is still there,
about half way between Manningtree and Ipswich.

Years pass - but here I am
on the same train,
with a baby on my lap,
going to show the in-laws
the first grandchild -
There it is!
Still there!

I live in the railway age.
The train goes on -

Stop! Stop!
Someone has cut down my tree!

Someone has pulled down the shelter
and dug up the spring.

The train goes on ...

Someone has pulled down the fence above and cut a great
swathe through the field. They're making a road!
Through My Field ...
You can't do THAT!

The train goes on.

Or do I live in the road age?

I have never yet set foot in MY FIELD -
But if I could find that road ...

I could - NOW!

1997

12

TRAVELLER

What is it to be a traveller?

Once, wandering through a wood,
I saw a spire of willowherb
Glow suddenly with intense meaning
Red, astonishing red luminosity.
        I could not look away.
Suddenly it glowed with absolute
        Being - being in itself;
            It was beauty, it was beyond beauty -
And then
        It was a spire of willowherb again.

To travel is to go
        On beyond the mountain ranges
            Through the deep woods, where, stumbling
                over a tree root in the green shadows,
a pool reflects my face ...
        and it is not me.

I know that I inhabit time in all its splendour -
but who knows where my future home will be?

Loveday - Bolton Abbey Oct '56

13

SNOW

Oh, in the north
      Don't the drifts heap, dividing
            Friend from friend, fresh falling, dividing
Me from you ?
      And we don't complain.
      Pile, sky, clouds greyly rolling
      On over lanes, hedges, roads
            till the heaps
      Drift, pile, heap higher and keep
            A sure wall, glinting, bright ...
                From hedge to hedge
                    between friend and friend.
Sleep.
      It's beautiful. Curling and rolling
      Sprayed, squeezed in creamy shapes,
      Like celestially narcotic trifle,
      It rears its blank impermeability.
            And I
                am cut off from you.
O snow
      Fighting slowly through comes the
            black and ugly
      Tractor, pulling the plough.
            Your empery wasn't long.
            We are together again.
                The snow has gone.

26.2.79

THE OLD CANAL

Under the bridge a blue canoe

Kingfisher blue
Flashes into the dark and through.

Over the bridge by the grey wall
   Under willow and alder
A child hides among the tall
Tangled weeds and ivy-fall
And pounces suddenly out...
A bicycle is pushed across
   Over and down the towpath;
The gravel crunches along the fosse,
Pebbles bounce down the green moss
   Into the dark cut.

Under the bridge a blue canoe -
   Kingfisher blue -
Flashes into the dark and through.

SOLITUDE

Solitude, I have sought you
    out where the trees end
and the endless trees begin.
Blackbirds scutter across the -
    suddenly startling across
      the dead grasses.
Blackbird?
    Did you see -
did you see solitude?
no no not here
    there are children calling
an old man smoking round the tombstones
    and a blackbird calls.

    Solitude?

Loch Ranza, I. of Aran
14.8.85

THE TELEPHONE

Is it you again, is it you?
   I thought it was - oh your incessant
      Demanding ring.
         Are you in? Am I through?
      Can I come?
         No you can't. Let's get it clear.
      I've got to go out, I'm deaf,
         I'm NOT HERE.

It rings again. There it goes again.
   I thought it would. Oh the unceasing
Requests, complaints, cries ...
         Shall I complain?
Go Ex-Directory?
         Cut it off? Not pay my bill?
It wastes hours of my time.
         <u>My</u> time - but still ...

Is time really mine? Mine to do what I like?
   I think, not really. It also belongs to you.
      Yes, I will listen ...
         Yes, you can come and talk.
   We must listen to each other - you have
      a right to my heart.
Without the lines between us, the world
      Will fall apart.

OWLS

Outside the house, out in the windy sky
I hear the owls reiterate their cry,
Kewick, Kewick, the little owls repeat,
Their soundless wings searching the viewless feet
Of tiny prey, scuttling from bush to clump
Of withered bracken round the broken stump.
Whoohoo, the barn owl says, on sweeping wing,
Quartering the wood, where no bird now can sing.

It is before the moon. Western and late,
The ragged robes of day disintegrate,
But at the zenith, in the deeper blue,
Orion and the Pleiades peep through.
It is before the dawn. For many hours
The world is yours, you owls;
It is not ours.
If we go out the trees will menace us,
The dark will fold its veil voluminous
And we, unwelcome as an unasked guest,
Go back uneasily, fears unconfessed.
Go back into the house, laugh, be at ease,
Do not stay here among the unfriendly trees.
We have the day, and many another song.
Do not stay here. This is where owls belong.

Under the moon may not man love and linger,
Watching the peaceful night touch with her finger
The gossamer filigree of umbel heads
Which nod their silver over mossy beds?
Now prowls the fox, and hails with angry bark
His rivals, stoats who also hunt the dark.
Now wails the bat, too shrill for mortal ear
But, fluttering low, brings the unwary fear.
No, do not linger out, now fades the light,
Now, say the owls, we are the folk of night.

THE BOAT

The boat,
      When I jump in, rocks.
      I push off and paddle,
      Driving it through the water,
         Standing up, rocking with the boat.

This thin glass shell
      Between me and the water
         Keeps me balanced,
            Free floating - rocking.

O pleasure of standing, rocking,
         Driving through the water!
      O white boat ...!

19

MONSTER

Going up Hellington Lane this morning
I met a monster.
It was chawing, clawing up the hedges
Breaking, destroying, churning up the earth.
And as it whirred and roared it
wept oily tears.
It spat out broken blackthorn branches.
Don't give me these spiky things it said
How can I digest them?
I have a terrible stomach ache already
I need oil, oil, oil.
And the telex tapped and the wires hummed
From Beirut to Bangladesh, from Bahrein to Bombay -
Sheiks chattered, oilrigs juddered,
Computers jammed in Houston, Texas -
He needs oil, oil, oil.

Then why have you destroyed the hedge,
monster? I said...
There was white foam along the lanes,
blackthorn, hawthorn,
Along the lanes in Claxton and Hellington and Rockland,
Bluebells, primroses, white foam of cow parsley,
And blackthorn, silver fountain of joy -
It won't grow again now you've broken it and clawed it.
Why did you do it?

But all he said was, weeping oily tears
And spitting out broken blackthorn branches,
I need oil, oil, oil.

Wires hummed, computers clacked, from
Ekofisk to Ekaterinburg.
Sheiks shuddered, peering at the oilwell levels,
Whispering : Nearly dry.

Look what you've done now,
I said to the monster,
You've used up all the oil and polluted
all the air,
And destroyed all the hedges that were
miracles of loveliness -
They won't grow again.

But his oily tears dropped on the devastated earth,
And all he said was, It wasn't my fault -
It wasn't _my_ fault - master.

Nov. 1979

USELESS...

Useless to bite one's nails and wonder Why
Did I do this? Where should I have been?
Now is the time, now is the only time
We live in - here is our only scene.
We are given no alternative.
Here and now we live.

Senseless the vague conditional questioning:
Should I have done it? Would it have been the same?
There is no alternative reality -
Here and unalterable is achievement, blame
And all that - in and out
Too quick to worry about.

In every moment there is to be done
Something - then or never again.
That only is what is needful to be known
And do, and pass, whether for joy or pain,
Putting the stitches in, time and tide -
The pattern's the other side.

1976

NO AFTERWARDS

When I see young mothers
Sitting by the sandpit in the park
Fall of hair over the smocked swell
Of coming hopes and troubles;
Calling, pushing on gloves, gossiping homeward
Ahead of coming dark -

Round them soft blown showers
Of sycamore leaves drifting the homeward routes
Of prams and trikes and skipping
Ropes, dogs sniffing the singly blooming
Lights, falling and blowing
Leaves scuffed by small red boots -

Then I know there is no afterwards
Of olding, scattering, thinning -
There are bare trees
There are old men on the seats
But the cold wind says
There is only beginning.

Autumn 1979

22

DREAMS

1. THE BATH

The water is green and deep
        and bubbles up within a porphyry basin.
        See them run and jump
            in,
garments left on the grass,
white in the sun. Green water gleams up
to embrace the naked flesh.
Oh how they dive, slide, splash,
        and, laughing,
        some swim, some glide beneath
        or throw up the crystal drops
        or, floating, lie and dream.
Come, they said, throw off those rags.
        The healing water waits.
No.
        No, I said, I can't, they're all I have
            to cover me.
        What, let you see my dust -
        and all these people?
Look, look, my feet are dusty,
And these are stains - I can't explain.
I'm crooked, besides, misshapen,
        (I didn't tell them that, but clutched the
        dirty cloak
            closer round me).
Take it off, they said,
        Look, you can't bathe with it on.
            No.
                I can't, I can't.
The green water,
        pure, and bright as an emerald,
            gleams as, crystal, it lips over
                to drop into the pool -
Let us help you, they said.
        Come, let us undress you.
        Shall I?

1978

HAY VINE

Hay vine
Hay a leary o
Grimskilly bilbarrow hay vine
       Lairy a merry o
Gree horris gree gree horris
       Skin wine sezzamally learyo
Skin wine tiltilly
          farrahay frack sezza lee
Sezzamally lair a merry
       Skin wine.
          Hay vine.

Grimslither grimslither grimslither kee
       Birryba rickity, bickity
Terryba reen, slen reden seen
       Voray a rugra, a reen.

Karry a rickity, grimslither kee
       Terryba reen, a reen
Maybo wayvo birryba rickity
       Rickity bibbity blink
          Bullomp, bullomp.

HERALDRY

Sometimes I see in my mind the scarlet lion
Ramping across the moonlit silver fields -
Trampling, the black stallion rears and yields
To the sinister bar, the cold rowels of iron.

Under the streaming pennants strewn with star
And moon, wheels to attack the bristly boar
Terribly blue; the spotted talbot, sore
From his gashes, lets the dogged fox run far.

Even the eagle, the gentle lamb, the shy
Unicorn, swan his strange gold collar rubs
Against domestic ploughs, crowns, jugs; cries
Down wind the royal white hart, lamenting stubs
Of lost old glories, now but swinging high
On creaking signs outside a thousand pubs.

Nov. 1978

Bamburgh Castle. Northumberland
June 1955

25

DREAMS

2. THE NEST

I remember the low timbered house,
With two rooms, that clung to the mountainside,
Backside to the wind, by a great rock.
        Pines sheltered it, wind-music soughing always
           Through them,
                Where, safe (they thought) a pair of
                  Goldcrests nested,
      Swinging on the springing bough.
        And I remember
The day I found the nest taken, trampled, rifled,
      Two eggs, crushed, spilling yolk on the path,
        One in his hand...the child's
While the bright birds cried and fluttered their
          Distress above him.
He looked at me and his eyes brimmed over;
      I think he had not meant -
        But I was angry and struck.
The red mark sprang and burned on his cheek.
      He looked at me.

JOURNEY

The old inn cradles us, warm and glowing;
In from the cold May evening, wet we came -
In from the dark miles of windy going
Dark rushing hedges backward flowing
      Mile after mile the same.

Berkshire cherry orchards ghostly gleaming,
Upland Cotswold fallows springing gold,
Cars striping the highway, black streaming
Across green Worcester, rain on Hereford teeming -
      In we came from the cold.

Here are soft voices, food and wine for the weary,
Lights glow, twinkle back from the old beams;
The red reflected fires in the mugs are cheery,
The ancient inn smells welcoming and beery
      And cradles us in dreams.

May 1973

Beck Hall. Malham.

April 1955

SONNET

Heartbreak, penury, bitter old age and pain,
All, all are entered on some office file,
Ticketed, numbered, punched, docketed, while
Some blank computer sicks them up again.
And even those whose bitter lives are thus
Swallowed and smoothed, learn a complete defence,
Armour themselves in shining steel pretence -
They do not grieve; they have no need to fuss.
How quickly we can learn, in time of grief
Or struggle, to regain content and ease -
Our wounds will heal, even if they are deep.
One tablet (in a drink) will bring relief
Shove thought and memory into the deep freeze -
We need not wake; better to stay asleep.

March 1979

PROPHETS

Do not mourn the vanished prophet, for
There are many conservative spokesmen still about
Who will trumpet forth conservative prophecies
Suitable to the established church.

But I would rather listen to Jesus -
A Radical if ever there was one -
So evidently not to be accounted a prophet...
(They said the same of Him when He was alive.)

THE PORT OF NORWICH, SUNDAY EVENING

Along the wharf ships rest, their muddy ropes
swinging and dipping to the oily heave.
No crews; they have gone gaily off on leave.

Idly, a single gull sweeps round in hopes
of crust or charity; one swan glides down
the muddy river, silent among the black
weed-covered piles, searching the floating wrack.

The angler packs his gear up. Noiseless, brown,
the river runs silently to the sea.
One bell chimes. Signalled, the hour shakes
to bells from castle hill, steeple and tower.

Suddenly evening wakens for an hour
As daylight fading leaves a last red streak -
bells wake the evening. Silence shakes.
Then quiet comes again...

Now for next week.

27.11.96

UNIVERSALS

If there is no
        Gold bright sunlight daisy
            But
                    only hawkbit, chamomile, and
                        that turned snake flake
                            bile -

If there are no
        Emerald deep waves
            or grass leaves
                but only frail reeds and
                    blistered paint -

If there is no
        Sky deep, cloud deep, azure
            pied
                shadow kingfisher's wing
      but only a
        birdseye speedwell and
            the sea -

If there are no royal hips, crimson haws,
        Flushed cheeks, strawberries,
           Fire,
                but only a pillar box
                  at the corner -

How come?

November 1978

YOU ARE THE SUN

You are the Sun.
>> Once, eight years old, I spun
>>> and danced on the steep grass
>>>> falling golden to the beechwood,
all among
>> bee orchids, clary and harebells
>>> ringing in the blue sky,
>>>> and I saw
>>>>> You in the sky.

Where
>> are you now?
In the hurrying feet
>> on the grey stones, in the street,
down the subway stairs?
>> Empty in the middle
is the world now, and the sky
>> is empty.

Empty in the middle
>> when I catch
>>> at the faces as they pass, and look
>>>> there!
>>>>> Oh *there* you are ...
I thought you'd gone.

You are the sun.
And I dance in the sun.

Jan. 1980

UNIVERSE

God took soap and water
    (He had thought of them first)
And then a pipe
    which He made of clay.
        (First He made the clay.)
Then He blew a bubble
    and the universe floated up, up, into the sunny air.
    Shiny, iridescent bubble ...
        aeons and galaxies and suns
        electrons, neutrons, protoplasm,
        electro-magnetic radiation, D.N.A.
        Pharaoh, Ptolemy, Popocatapetl,
        Khmer and Ming
        and the moth's wing
        and everything you can think of, everything ...
And then the bubble burst.
    So God laughed and blew
        and myriads, myriads of iridescent bubbles
        floated up.. full of joy, full of God's laughter ...
            all new ...

16.12.96

IN A COUNTRY CHURCH

There is nobody in the church
                no one at all.
          The organ creaks;
dust dances in the azure light from the Virgin's robe in the
          east window.
The old hassocks lie askew, dusty and humble,
          a smell of ancient piety,
                silence.

There is nobody here
                no one at all.
          Clean stone, stained walls, old crooked timbers
                    listen ...
     and hush -
                in the expectant, dusty silence Someone
                    speaks.

Rockland
June 1974

33

VOWELS

Black A, white E, red I, green U, blue O, - vowels
One day I will reveal your hidden cry
A, black corselet of the shining fly
Bombing around cruel earth's bowels

Shadowed abyss; E, vaporous candour of tents
Proud glacier's light, white kings, wild parsley a-tremble;
I, crimson spilt blood, lips smiling to dissemble
In anger or in drunken penitence.

U, cycles, vibrations of viridian seas, divine
Peace of a countryside of folded kine,
The studious frown of alchemy's surmise ...
O, supreme clarion, strange azure hurled
Silences traversing angels and world -
O the Omega, blue glance of His eyes!

(after Rimbaud)
16.12.96

STILL MORE ...

Still more if all is darkness and silence
hard rock
steep way
path leading nowhere -
still more in black night must the traveller listen
for the distant cockcrow that heralds the dawn.

All there is the weary plodding
step after faint step
stumbling and falling,
at the last at a standstill in the darkness
all there is black night as the traveller listens,
despairing hope, the chill wind of dawn.

Not yet a lightening far off on the horizon,
breeze bending -
grass greening -
gilded sunrising -
all there is travelling, travelling, in darkness.
Still more in silence must the traveller listen -
for the distant cockcrow that heralds the dawn.

Oct. 7th 1988

WEEKEND

Written after a weekend with the Sacred Dance Group in Dorset

Friday Evening

Here is this shining floor for me to display
Myself, cavort, turn and glide -
And I find instead
I want to hide.
Why can't I sing and leap and rejoice
Free, like you others, free to be,
To love, to laugh, to live,
free to be me?

Why am I stiff, reluctant, cold?
Oh look, now we've got to make sandpies ...
How foolish - how ...
Making sandpies - for that I am too old.
That's why mine won't -
Why look - it WON'T ...
make.
It crumbles - try again - no ...
DAMN IT, stay together, will you - ?
No ...

Well, Lord, I can't help seeing, it's quite
clear there's a great hard lump of clay
or something in my sand - but do
I want a sandpie anyway?

Saturday morning

Empty space, one candle flame -
Gathering silently, expectantly,
we turn towards
that impelling breath ...
lifting clods, stones, shapeless lumps of clay
and feeling fingers form,
spread, clutch, twine together ...
an unseen Hand moulding the tensile thumb
tracing the netted palm.
Now!
Left free by the creating Hand I lift,
Clap, throw ...
and clutch - and hit.
Anger informs the self-directed hands
so lately raised in joy.

But look...
>Over there we can lay down these heavy stones
by the Cross and lift our spoiled hands
>under the cleansing blood.

Saturday Afternoon

A weary waste seems this way,
>This afternoon, heavy to hear,
Slow to tread.
Reluctant though I am to go this way,
I must retrace, along the empty floor
>The backward steps
>>Into dread.
Down into the dark of what I have forgotten
And what I would like to forget -
>Very deep in ...
Into the hurt of past hurt and grief
>and sin.

O my little ones, and my loved ones,
>I have hurt you, and I must remember
>>and weep over your pain.

But look ...
>One walks this road
>Who bears a heavy load
>And I may walk beside and carry it too.

Here is healing, here is gain for all loss
>under Your Cross.

Saturday Evening

Tears flow free
>from a source
very deep, below
>all outerly I know ...
from some dark well of being
>that is me.

Tears flow, profound
>fountains of grief
from the abyss below.
Those hard stones crumble
>and the healing streams
>>flow.

Sunday Morning

Now the shining floor
        is ploughland, waiting
                the fallen grain.
Hidden, it lies
        silent, receiving
                God's sun and rain.
Let not the hidden barriers
        be raised to keep you out -
                You, and my human kin -
Let not masks hide me,
        gates be shut against You -
                Open, I ask You in.

Sunday Afternoon

Singing and dancing,
        Come we together,
                To praise, to rejoice, we come.
Friends, God speed, goodbye.
        Thanking Him, thanking you,
                Out into the rainy weather
                      We go home.

TOLLUND MAN

The little man lies under glass
Lies with his black, wrinkled face;
His leather belt is still in place;
The crowds press round him, gaze and pass.

So peaceful-looking, no sad wreck,
It looks as if without a cry,
As the noose tightened round his neck,
He dropped on to the moss to die.

Perhaps he simply cocked his eye,
Under his pointed leather cap,
Up at the clouds, and thought - poor chap -
I've had it but I don't know why.

And then under the bog he lay
Two thousand years; they dug him up,
And now he lies in Silkeborg,
In a glass case, and has his say -

Speechless he says to the tourists crowding by:
Look at me; we are human, you and I.

FACADE

(SAN MINIALTO AL MONTE, FLORENCE)

Alberti measured, thought, scribbled and cut,
Divided, reasoned, argued out the whole -
How three by four should signify the soul
And two on top of seven should sound it out.
And here it stands, perfect in black and white,
Miniatured loveliness, for future time
To learn from through the centuries; sublime
Architect's model, reasoned thought's delight.
But go inside. In there the ancient stone,
The barrelled gloom, dim light through tracery sprayed,
The struggling aeons as the faithful prayed,
Open on to a timeless end unknown.
Alberti's genius made the pretty face
Outside; within find the deep fount of grace.

Wensum Lodge
March 1979

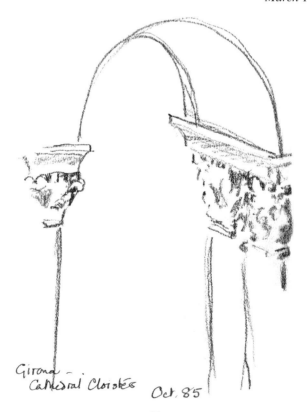

Girona -.
Cathedral Cloisters   Oct. 85

HERE I AM

Here, I
           am ...
What does it mean, I?
Under the vast and empty sky,
      A shreds-and-patches thing -
      An infinitesimal, lonely cry -
           I.

Here, I
           wait ...
What am I waiting for?
Down the trails of an empty universe
      Echoes the pop of a puncture -
      There goes the tyre of the hearse ...

I am a meeting
         with no friend.
I am a game
         with no goal.
I am a road
         with no end ...
      There is no answer.

I AM that I AM.

No name?
      This is so large an I
      I am afraid.
This is an end-game all one.

This is no game -
      and I have not won.

Knowledge unontological
      And concept inconceivable,
         Beyond all size magnifical
           And real beyond all thought.

How can I know you?
How can I love you?
      You are not my sort.

But how do I know that
When I don't know what sort I am?
      Under the empty sky
      A lonely cry -

And there was an answer after all -
      There was a call ...
      A call for me to answer -

Lord, here am
         I.

7.7.75

COMMUNICATION

A SESTINA

Incoming calls we get, but there's a humming
And suddenly it rings - there's no-one there -
Yes, we've told them - several times we've said,
Rung up and said, and the engineer's been coming
Several times - probably we were out.
No, we've had no complaints.

But oh, far lovers', children's, friends' complaints
Would never reach our ears for all their coming.
With this darn bell, ringing when no-one's there,
How do we know what thunderous moans are humming
Over the wires, and will to be let out?
One wants to know, when all is said and done.

For after all, there's so much to be said,
People are always ringing, with complaints,
Or funny or alarming news, which there,
In their place, seems to be wanting to burst out.
We want to listen, too, I tell you; humming
A hymn, or leaving the milk to boil, we're coming

To pick it up, curious to know what's coming,
Who's rung. And then it's that old nobody there.
Old nobody, we don't want your complaints -
People may want us - what was that you said?
I can't hear properly with all this humming -
Nobody's ringing up again. Get out.

Listen, listen. It's we who are always out
When somebody wants to unburden bitter complaints.
Unwatched, the milk boils over. The baker's coming.
Over the shaggedy lawn the mower's humming.
Someone, or no-one with something important, said
We never heard because we were not there.

Trying so hard to get us, Somebody there -
Who? Tried and tried to get you, he said,
But we turned away from his wearying complaints
And said, There's nobody there - We keep on coming
And every time we get this funny humming.
Nobody said - They're out.

The engineer kept telling us he was coming
Several times - but probably we were out.
No, we've no complaints.

1976

42

DAWN

Early, early wakes the van of dawn.
A bird chirps, a lorry grinds its gears -
Then fly, my heart, to the paling East to pray
To ease my burden of my night-time fears.
Anxious and desolate, the chances those
I love are bound to face oppress my mind;
This one perhaps sick, that lonely, and the woes
(far worse) of those who have left You behind.
But see, the cloud flushing towards the dawn,
As You, my glorious sun, flood all my sky
With love and praise and the knowledge that forlorn
and sad, nearer than prosperous am I,
You nearer me, and my beloved than sight -
And, what is more, You were near us all the night.

Sept. 1973

Boats at Skei
28.8.71

BRIGHTWELL

Parish Communion nine-fifteen on Sunday
morning at St. Agatha's,
Sunday School at eleven o'clock in the Rectory Room,
staggering across with paste-pot balanced on a
pile of books,
large roll of paper flapping
round my ear, joy joy joy ...
Monday is school again, wiping stickies all morning,
Monday is Brownies.
Tuesday is dustbin day, dustbin, dustbin
dustbin day.
Calloo, callay, O dustbin day!
Put out more dustbins, darling!
Dustbins, dustbins, run with dustbins
on Tuesday, and Wednesday is
earlyclosingday.
I have forgotten to buy bread,
eggs,
sugar, tea, oranges...
and it is Wednesday,
Earlyclosingday.
Thursday is M.U.,W.I., you name it we have it,
Friday is Guides,
Saturday is "shall we go down to the boats?
no we must dig the garden"
and suddenly
Ding Ding Ding, there go the ringers -
it is Saturday evening again and soon it will be
nine-fifteen on Sunday at St. Agatha's.

O God I want something different.
Lord, they say You are always the same -
Is it true, I wonder?
Yes, I suppose You are always the same
and yet I think
You are also always
different.

May 1973

ADVENT ONE

Now in the time of this mortal life
Now is the time to do the Christmas shopping -
I saw him with three bottles of wine
                                under his arm,
Two of sherry (his wife had the brandy
                                in her pocket).
It was easy, they didn't have to pay,
The cashier was looking the other way.

I saw the kids, with huge gay boxes
And greedy eyes, coming down the street,
Greedy voices whining, Gimme, gimme,
Can I have Action Man? Can I have a bike?
The horse-leech isn't the only man alive
Who has four daughters (and sons) crying
                                Give! Give!

And how am I going to manage? said Mrs. Bailey,
Shuffling across the cold room to light a candle -
The power-men are on strike again
And they say there'll be a bread shortage -
He's incontinent - he's old, you see -
And I can't manage the washing -
                                I'm eighty-three.

Now in the time of this mortal life
Now in this time of misery and darkness
Now is the time to get up, to arise and go,
Light one candle and journey, not knowing where ...
We have no power, no bread, and no star ...
To start we must take one step from where we are.

Now in the time of this mortal life,
As the year turns to the long night,
Give us grace to cast off the works of darkness,
And put upon us the armour of light.

December 1977

MOTHERING SUNDAY

I'll bring you a cuppa tea in bed, Mum.
You stay in bed and I'll cook the joint.
Or you can get up and sit around all morning,
As long as you don't do anything, that's the point.

Oh, here you are, Mum, making tea -
I never woke up; but just you sit about.
I'll put the meat in as soon as I'm dressed
And do the spuds after I've just popped out.

What a lovely dinner, Mum, just as usual.
Sorry I never got back to cook it, it was because..
Sit down when you've washed up;
                    I'll get you some flowers tomorrow -
        (That is - I'm skint, but if I could just borrow)
Cos you're the very best Mum there ever was.

1979

46

ANGLICAN DIVERSITY

If you want to experience the Anglican Church in all its varied diversity,
Come down into the ** Group of a fine Sunday morning;
As long as the ministering team aren't hit by unusual scurcity,
(Such as a tummy-bug laying them all low without any warning.)*

There are brasses and rood-screens and poppyheads and fonts
Elaborate chancels and plain;
There are thatched roofs and tiled roofs and high roofs and low ,
And one that lets in the rain.

There are organs that squeak and organs that moan,
The tunes may be fetched from afar;
There may be (and often is) no organist at all,
Or else there is Bob-and-guitar.

So gird up your mental powers and be ready for anything,
You may have to scale the mystic heights with Julian of Norwich;
You may have to leap up and down, clap your hands and do that
        sort of funny thing,
Or you may find yourself released (because the chap's got to go
        on to the next one)
In thirty minutes flat to your porridge.

One of them is roughly, but not very, in the high direction,
One of them is nautical, and may be aground on a lee shore far
        down the Yare;
The lay Reader is middling, and nobody can understand what he's on about,
One's charismatical, so you never know what to expect when he's there.

It might be Series 3 at top speed,
It might be 1662 and very slow,
It might be no-one knows what, totally drowned by
        infant voices ...
You just *never know.*

So venture into the ** Group and take the luck of the pot;
The joke is, you never know WHICH church is having WHAT ...

*This really did happen once

WENSUM LODGE

Said Simon Lovett as he scratched his nose
The winter day is drawing to a close.
But Peter Bullock spat into the fire
And added: Now a pint is my desire.
The wind is rushing, beating at the door,
And we have beer and bread and cheese and more.
Not so, said Simon, for we have no beer,
We must send Philip out for it, I fear.
Not me, said Philip Hogsnye as he spat
Neatly into the hearth from where he sat.
For I paid last time, and I quite refuse
Thus to be subject to a mean abuse.
Go fetch your own beer, Simon, if you must
And if you won't, then crumble all to dust.
I'll see you further, jiminy, so I will,
(Only it wasn't jiminy) said Phil.
Simon leered round, and stretched a hefty fist
Under Phil's nose, and loudly said: Desist!
It wasn't me, but Peter, asked for drink,
For I have something better here, I think.
Whereon he looked into a press of oak,
Peering in rheumily through fog and smoke,
And then withdrew, all wreathed in smiles again,
Held proudly up a bottle of Champagne!
Come on, said Peter, that's a cheering sight;
We won't care now how stormy grows the night.
And even Philip cheerfully will go,
Surely, to put some glasses in a row.
He's right, for as he spoke the deed was done;
The glasses winked; the oaken table shone.
The fire burned high, glittered the knife and fork,
And sudden from the bottle popped the cork.
Oh then, what tales, what songs, what laughter roars!
All is good company and mirth indoors,
While outside, battering at the door in vain,
The wind moans: Hey, I've no Champagne!
They kept it up until the night was gone
And outside palely broke the winter dawn.
He had some more Champagne, I haste to say,
And even Philip didn't have to pay.

Wensum Lodge
11.3.79

ROCKLAND ST MARY I

Rock-hard the soil here, and the little children

Skip, twirl from end to end of the village street
Like tadpoles wriggling between shop and shop.

The little white shop sells crisps and refreshers
The little red shop sells crisps and ices;

Here wander the homegoing prams, and stop.

Oh pink the ices, cold and sweet the lard,
Oh red the little houses, cold and hard.

Marshy the fields lap against the headland
Of New Inn Hill, where cycling down the children
Fish from the staithe, calling each to each.

And the boat-people, strangers from distant places,

Stroll up the street on Sundays, sucking ices -

Here wander they, as on a foreign beach.

Oh red the little houses, cold and hard,
Empty the marl pits, hollow and rubbish-marred.

Digging, building, watering, frozen fathers
Fight for the children's future, crisps and ices

From one shop to the other shop.

All down the street wriggle the tadpole children,
Shrilly calling, licking the cold sweet ices -

All down the street the toffee papers drop.

Oh red the little houses, cold and hard.
Hollow the hammers in the builder's yard.

May 1976

ROCKLAND ST. MARY II

Here in Rockland St. Mary there is gold
Spilling over the fields out of the sky,
Great sausages, blocks of gold rolled
All summer long - wheat and barley high
Over little Anne's head where she walks through;
So much gold winter won't run dry.
Do you believe me? You should. It's true.

Richness of brown shiny conkers here
Spill from spiky husks for Steve and Paul,
Handfuls of conkers for Andrew to share
With little Danny, who finally gets them all.
Andrew lives up in a big old yew;
Steve and Barry have a monster ball.
Do you believe me? You should. It's true.

Here in Rockland sugar candy's a crop,
Farmer Alec digs rivers and makes a bridge
Between the willow stump and the alder top -
You can see a forest of masts over the ridge.
And the wicked old heron and the bittern, too,
Fish down there to rob poor Alec's fridge.
Do you believe me? You should. It's true.

Only last Sunday there was this great pike
Jumped right out of the water and Splash! Splat!
There he was in the canoe with Mike,
Slopping about right where he was sat
Those great fierce teeth - it's only a small canoe...
You should have seen how quick he got out of that.
Do you believe me? You should. It's true.

Autumn 1978

NOVEMBER

November's zebra beauty hides its grace,
Hides it in striped plough and the crusted pillars
After the first snow, along the wood.
Shadows and dazzle jacquard the banked lane.
Shy, not proud or brash, this beauty,
As gay December decks its berried hedge,
Or harsh fire strikes from frozen pools in January.
      Billow in glory now
Soft clouds of tawny gold from the ribbed trunks,
Not bared yet to the cold stripping wind,
But veiled in colour or in cloud, when quiet
The first frost yields again to wreathing mist.
Down rutted lanes the starveling blackbirds scatter,
The winter twilight softly drops to dark,
Leaving to die the sky's last glowing ember ...
      This is November.

November 1978

IN THE SAME BOAT

You jump on, she lurches perilously,
I hand the engine in, the oars, the food -
Primary this - we can't up anchor, catch
The wind aloft, swing round the willow, fly
Hungry down tide, and empty wait the flood.

You hoist the sails - shout "Mind the Bishop's paint!"
I take the tiller, wary eye on trees
That stretch across the dyke to stop our way
Out, round the reeds, the creaking blocks' complaint
Tells that the sail pulls to the welcome breeze.

Up river come the coasters, laden from sea,
Among the reeds grebe families dive and float,
Terns scream above - the heron heavy flaps
Across, as we drift home in time for tea -
On shore again,
But still in the same boat.

Rockland

Oban 11.6.84

ABOVE SALTHOUSE

We lay on the warm curve of land's shoulder,
My love and I, rupescent of blackberries.
Heather-warmed bees' gold song murmuring to curlews,
Sandpipers on the far sand crying the tide -

Gently curves the sea round saltmarsh and shingle,
Gently-running creeks wandering through sea-lavender,
Little boats playing.

High hangs in pale emptiness a kestrel,
So still, so sculptured on the void morning.

Still bird ...
Gentle sea ...
They are waiting to destroy.

BIRTHDAY

Love life, love all,
Harvest field and golden cream and love in bed,
Waves breaking down the shingle,
Grass bending, clouds dancing,
O and a single
       Spire of willowherb, intensest red,
          Holding the key to all.

And love the holding
Of babies, warm and soft, who look with eyes
       Changed to critics, disappearing
          And appearing through a thousand crises
Of scorn and cheering -
       When love sinks low, a new surprise
          Springs new, new love unfolding.

And love pain,
The learning of grief and fears and tears alone,
       Heart squeezed in, no solace, only
          This is how it is, that's all.
And all the lonely
       Learning, that this is all to call one's own -
          At the end, this is all.

Love death,
For here spring life and light, to birth again
       In dark, in silence and in naughting,
          The most peremptory nullification
             Of self, of love, of all.
Here is salvation.
       In loss, in loneliness, in grief and pain
          Is life again.

Sept.13th.1973

A 303

I really feel I must resist
The idea that I do not exist;
Also my mind firmly repels
The notion that I'm someone else.

But when I gaily say: My Mind ...
What sense in that can thinkers find?
And surely my pretension's high
To think I know that I am I.

Oh, am I I? Or am I not?
Have I a mind or body got?
And when it comes to brassiest tacks
Am I a being what can ax?

And when I've axed these questions few
What meaning can attach thereto -
Seeing you think I think I mean
Something quite else than what I do?

My grammar's gone, my mind's awıy,
And anyway I am not I
Boil up the kettle, make the tea -
Write and withdraw from 303.

March 1975

THE KYMIN

As I lay on the Kymin a cuckoo was shouting,
        The air hummed, heat lay on the hill,
Wind bent the silver grass, rustled the birches, .
        The distant farms lay still.
And I thought of freedom, and sorrow, and men who die,
    As the cuckoo shouted in the woods above the Wye.

As I lay on the Kymin the oak leaves whispered,
        Haze shimmered in the blue valleys of Dean,
A wind blew from the distant hills of Brecon
        And over the leagues between -
Here men have fought, and sorrowed - and here I lie,
    As the cuckoo shouts in the woods above the Wye.

5.6.74

DREAMS

3. THE MESSAGE

I was alone when he came into the hall,
A dark presence. I stood up. His shadow
frightened me, but he said
>   Ride. Take the dark horse and ride with this message
>   Ride with it to the castle. Do not go in
>   unless they tell you to.
>   I was afraid - I had not ridden
since I was a child, but the black horse was gentle
and let me mount.
>   Down forest rides, through the ranked boles
>   we rode like the wind, and the trees
>   came up like armies round us, and broke rank
>   and melted away, and came again.
>   In the silence the hoofs thudded,
>   dark and silence grew round us.
Then the path was steep.
>   I knew we were going up, and once,
>   suddenly in the starlight, the edge of the path
>   fell away and I saw,
>   far, far below, a town with lights
>   glimmering round a dark lake...
>   but so far below, so far, I felt faint...
>   it was only a glimpse.
>   Then I felt the black horse
>   slip and struggle on the stones, and then
>   we were over the crest, I knew by the feel...
>   over the top of the pass, we were going down again.
I heard how his hoofs thudded again
on a grassy ride, and the trees closed round.
Suddenly in front of us there were steps
and a door with yellow lamplight streaming from it,
people going in and out, crowds of people.
I gave my letter to someone standing by the door.
>   He took it with a smile.
>   He did not ask me to come in.
He took it in, and I waited, leaning
>   by the black horse.
Presently he came out and gave me another letter,
>   and smiled. He said nothing.
But as I mounted and turned my horse's head,
through the black forest and up the mountain paths,
his remembered smile was a fire and a bliss
>   in my head, and I thought
it was worth so long a journey.
When I dismounted the dark shadowy presence was waiting.
>   I gave him the letter.
Rub your horse down, he said, before you sleep.
I was glad to find the stables and the rubber, and, yawning,
to rub him down while he nuzzled my shoulder -
glad to see there was hay in the manger.
>   Glad to sleep.

1978

THE EARTH-MOVER

I passed this morning on my way
in to Norwich between Bramerton
and Kirby Bedon, an earth-mover,
yellow, immense, its jaws grinding -
already it had eaten a huge hole
in a beet field.

Under the unimpressed sky,
yellow and solitary, it chawed and chumped.
By the time we came back in the afternoon
it had eaten down into the Yare valley.
Schlooping, it nibbled Brundall away and
digested Cantley with pleasure ...
(sweet, sweet sugar beet -)
Yarmouth disappeared, big wheel and little wheels ...
and the sea, its waves yellowing,
came frisking up the disappearing land.

The earth-mover swallowed the sea.
Then Rotterdam, Hamburg, Uppsala -
somebody's heels stuck up in Tomsk
then glup, glub,
Beijing had gone and Tokyo
Alaska, New York;
finally the earth-mover
yellow, solitary, jaws moving ruminatively,
ate up
          itself.

28.11.96

THREE BOATS

Three bright plastic boats were set afloat
By Simeon and me
Two were red and blue, and one small boat
Bobbed red and green down to the open sea.

Bright red and blue, swirling along the tide,
They bobbed and tossed,
Turning, dipping, round the tough rocks they ride.
Two came safe to the shore - but one was lost.

At sunset down by the sea a bright red speck
Amazed I saw,
Riding the foam triumphantly, no wreck,
The little red boat was tossed again on shore.

How many heavy hearts each eventide
Helplessly stand
And watch the little boats drift out to sea
And weep. Yet somewhere, though far off it be,
Those little boats come safe again to land.

At Lee Abbey
May 1989

Bretton -
May 1989

FOX

Sun brilliant on the white mist
Joy brims the early valley
as white mist brims the valley, brilliant with sun.

He looked at me from the edge of the clearing
Brown like the bracken
He had jumped up
Just now as my foot scattered the dew -
Jumped away, turned, froze still and looked at me.

At the other side of the clearing
Ears pricked, brown in the brown bracken,
He stopped and looked at me.
Prick ears, white belly; dark questing eyes
Look into mine from twenty yards away.

Your fear mirrors mine; I am a fugitive too
From critical frowns and clumsy feet that brush away the dew.
Free, you jump away, vanish in the bracken; you are gone.

I find your freedom in the joy you gave me.

Wydale
Dec.1979

FEBRUARY

Brown striped plough away down the
hollow fields to the smoke grey trees -
lies quiescent, silent, lifeless -
waiting.

Ribbed grey trunk of the ash at the
corner of the steel grey water -
lifts its crooked aspiring branches -
waiting.

Under earth, under bark, under time, the
returning breath of living -
trembles into green leaf, white petal -
waking.

Rockland 1974

WHEN ONE SAYS YES

When one says yes
To love's demand by wing-light
Then in the nine months' darkness grows
Time's miracle, a winter rose -
And comes in the bitter air
To birth - ah, see
The child his mother hushes.

When one says yes
To journeying road by starlight
Unmapped, the rugged road leads straight
To high-swung sign and open gate;
Travelling men may share
Pure peace in the low house -
Music, the evening thrushes.

When one says yes
To labouring days by noonlight
Blistered hands and aching back
Build in the desert a king's track;
Wayfaring fools walk there
Safe on the cockatrice' den -
There are pools among the rushes.

Nov. 1978 and 2.12.96

Lindisfarne 3.8.87